THE WORLD'S BIOMES

Deserts

THE WORLD'S BIOMES

Deserts

Grasslands

Oceans

Rainforests

Wetlands

THE WORLD'S BIOMES

Deserts

Kimberly Sidabras

MASON CREST
PHILADELPHIA

Mason Crest
450 Parkway Drive, Suite D
Broomall, PA 19008
www.masoncrest.com

© 2019 by Mason Crest, an imprint of National Highlights, Inc.

Printed and bound in the United States of America.

CPSIA Compliance Information: Batch #B2018.
For further information, contact Mason Crest at 1-866-MCP-Book.

First printing
1 3 5 7 9 8 6 4 2

Library of Congress Cataloging-in-Publication Data

Names: Sidabras, Kimberly, author.
Title: Deserts / Kimberly Sidabras.
Description: Philadelphia : Mason Crest Publishers, 2019. | Series: The world's biomes | Includes bibliographical references and index. |
  Identifiers: LCCN 2017048387 (print) | LCCN 2017057777 (ebook) | ISBN 9781422277515 (ebook) | ISBN 9781422240366 (hardcover)
Subjects: LCSH: Deserts—Juvenile literature. | Desert ecology—Juvenile literature.
Classification: LCC GB612 (ebook) | LCC GB612 .S53 2019 (print) | DDC 577.54—dc23
LC record available at https://lccn.loc.gov/2017048387

THE WORLD'S BIOMES series ISBN: 978-1-4222-4035-9

QR CODES AND LINKS TO THIRD-PARTY CONTENT

Table of Contents

1: What Is a Desert? 7
2: How Life Exists in a Desert.............................21
3: The Benefits of Deserts 33
4: The Threat to Deserts 41
5: Addressing the Desertification Problem 57

Quick Reference: Deserts...............................66
Appendix: Climate Change 68
Series Glossary of Key Terms 72
Further Reading 74
Internet Resources 75
Index 77
Photo Credits/About the Author 80

KEY ICONS TO LOOK FOR:

Words to understand: These words with their easy-to-understand definitions will increase the reader's understanding of the text while building vocabulary skills.

Sidebars: This boxed material within the main text allows readers to build knowledge, gain insights, explore possibilities, and broaden their perspectives by weaving together additional information to provide realistic and holistic perspectives.

Educational Videos: Readers can view videos by scanning our QR codes, providing them with additional educational content to supplement the text. Examples include news coverage, moments in history, speeches, iconic sports moments and much more!

Text-dependent questions: These questions send the reader back to the text for more careful attention to the evidence presented there.

Research projects: Readers are pointed toward areas of further inquiry connected to each chapter. Suggestions are provided for projects that encourage deeper research and analysis.

Series glossary of key terms: This back-of-the-book glossary contains terminology used throughout this series. Words found here increase the reader's ability to read and comprehend higher-level books and articles in this field.

 Words to Understand

alluvial fan—a fan-shaped layer of sand and gravel laid down by water.

arid—used to describe an area with less than 25 cm of annual rainfall.

arroyo—a temporary watercourse in an American desert that fills only after rare rainstorms.

dormant—describes animals or plants in which all life processes have almost stopped, usually until warmth or water wakes them up, sometimes after years.

oasis—a fertile spot in a desert, supplied with underground water.

playa lake—a lake in a hot region that has no drainage stream, which collects water that then evaporates in the hot climate.

precipitation—natural water that falls from the sky in the form of rain, snow, sleet, hail, dew, frost and fog.

transpiration—the loss of water vapor from plant leaves.

wadi—a temporary watercourse in a North African or Arabian desert that fills only after rare rainstorms (the same as an American arroyo).

What Is a Desert?

A person asked to describe a desert would probably use words such as "sandy," "flat," "hot," and "lifeless." Yet deserts are not necessarily sandy, are often hilly, are sometimes cold, and are hardly ever completely without life.

Scientists define a desert as a region that loses more water into the air as water vapor than it receives as *precipitation* in the form of rain, snow, sleet, hail, dew, or frost. Deserts lose water as vapor in two ways. When water is heated by the sun it begins to evaporate, or turn to vapor. Plants also soak up water at their roots and breathe it out as vapor, in a process called *transpiration*.

Arid deserts receive less than 10 inches (25 cm) of precipitation each year. There is hardly any cloud above them during the day, and the sun heats the desert surface very quickly. The dry desert air cannot hold onto this heat at night, which is why desert nights can be bitterly cold. Very cold regions of the Arctic and the Antarctic are called polar deserts. They are extremely dry throughout the year because all their moisture is locked up in ice.

There are often semi-arid regions fringing the arid deserts, where precipitation ranges between 10 and 35 inches (25 and 90 cm) each year. These are the areas where unsuitable farming methods and native plant destruction are most likely to turn the land to desert.

Different Types of Desert

All deserts are arid, but they are arid for different reasons. There are four main processes that create deserts and keep them that way, and so there are four types of desert. They are horse-latitude deserts, continental deserts, rain-shadow deserts, and coastal deserts.

Biome versus Ecosystem

A biome is a very large ecological area, with plants and animals that are adapted to the environmental conditions there. Biomes are usually defined by physical characteristics—such as climate, geology, or vegetation—rather than by the animals that live there. For example, deserts, rainforests, and grasslands are all examples of biomes. Plants and animals within the biome have all evolved special adaptations that make it possible for them to live in that area.

A biome is not quite the same as an ecosystem, although they function in a similar way. An ecosystem is formed by the interaction of living organisms within their environment. Many different ecosystems can be found within a single biome. Components of most ecosystems include water, air, sunlight, soil, plants, microorganisms, insects, and animals. Ecosystems exist on land and in water, with sizes ranging from a small puddle to an enormous swath of desert.

Surrounded by a desert of salt flats, Utah's Great Salt Lake supports a number of salt-resistant animals like the brine shrimp, as well as the birds and other creatures that feed on them.

The world's largest deserts, including the Sahara, the Arabian Desert, and the Australian Desert, lie roughly 30°N or 30°S of the Equator, in the so-called "horse latitudes." Air heated up at the Equator rises, loses its moisture, and descends over these latitudes, becoming hot winds which dry up any moisture.

Continental deserts, such as the Gobi Desert of Mongolia and China, lie in the center of the large landmasses we call continents, far from the oceans which are the source of all rainfall.

Rain-shadow deserts form near mountain ranges that cut

them off from the sea. Moisture-laden air currents moving inland from oceans cool down when they rise up the slopes of these mountain barriers, and release all their moisture as rain. The dry air warms up as it flows down the opposite side of the mountains. It evaporates any local moisture, forming deserts such as America's Mojave Desert, east of the Sierra Nevada mountains.

Coastal deserts form near oceans with cool ocean currents. The air above these currents is also cool, and loses its moisture as rain at sea. The cool, dry air moves inland and creates deserts such as the Namib Desert of southwest Africa along-side the cool Benguela Current, and the Atacama Desert of south Peru and northern Chile, caused by the cool Humboldt Current.

The World's Major Deserts

The world's largest deserts are not areas that are traditionally thought of as being desert, but they do fit the definition. Antarctica, which receives less than eight inches (20 cm) of precipitation annually at the coasts, and far less inland, is home to the world's largest and driest desert, covering most of the continent. It is also the coldest desert, reaching temperatures of $-81°F$ ($-63°C$) and below. The Antarctic desert covers roughly 5.5 million square miles (14 million square kilometers).

There are also polar deserts in the northern Arctic regions, including parts of Alaska, as well as Canada, Greenland, Iceland, Norway, Sweden, Finland, and Russia. The Arctic deserts cover about the same area as the Antarctic desert.

Powerful desert winds loaded with mineral particles constantly wear away at rocky surfaces, removing any loose fragments to reshape rocks such as these pinnacles in the Algerian Sahara.

Educational Video

For an overview of deserts and the animals that live there, scan here:

The Sahara is the world's largest "hot" desert. It stretches across fourteen North African countries, with a total area of well over 3.3 million square miles (9 million sq. km). There are huge areas of sand, but over two-thirds of the Sahara consists of features such as gravel plains, and mountains tall enough to have winter snows.

The Arabian Desert, which is located in region of western Asia commonly known as the Middle East, is the sandiest of the great deserts. At its heart is the pure sand desert known as the Empty Quarter. This grim, inhospitable area, usually entered only by local Bedouin people, contains huge, ancient dunes. It covers more than 900,000 square miles (2.33 million sq. km).

The Gobi Desert of Mongolia and northern China is a region of high, waterless steppes and stone-littered plains, which suffers blistering summer heat and frozen winters. This region covers approximately 500,000 square miles (1 million sq. km).

The North American Desert is a combination of four major desert areas. It ranges from the valleys and dunes of the semi-desert Great Basin, through the mountains and dried lakes of the Mojave Desert, and the cactus-studded plains of the Sonoran Desert; finally it reaches the shrubby desert lands of the Chihuahua Desert in Mexico.

The few San Bushmen who still live in their traditional way in Namibia's Kalahari Desert often travel great distances on foot in pursuit of game.

The Kalahari Desert is located at the heart of southern Africa. It varies between red sand dunes and semi-arid grasslands, and contains the Okavango Delta, Africa's largest *oasis*—the remains of a huge prehistoric lake. The Kalahari stretches across an area of 360,000 square miles (900,000 sq. km), including parts of the countries of Angola, Botswana, Namibia, and South Africa.

The Namib Desert is a 1,200-mile (2000-km) long coastal desert: a mix of shifting dunes, rock and gravel plains. Sea fogs provide scarce moisture for plants and animals, and rainfall is no more than 8 inches (20 cm) per year.

The Australian Desert covers a large part of the continent's "outback." Some 70 percent of Australia receives less than 500 mm of rain per year, and 18 percent of the country is true desert. There are four major deserts in the western part of the continent: the Great Sandy Desert, the Gibson Desert, the Great Victoria Desert, and the Simpson Desert.

The Atacama Desert on the western side of the Andes in South America is another coastal desert. It is the world's driest desert apart from Antarctica.

The Patagonian Desert is a high-altitude, cold-winter rain-shadow desert. It extends from the Andes mountains almost to the Atlantic, down the length of Argentina and into Chile.

The Thar Desert of India and Pakistan once contained fertile river valleys, until a change of wind direction moved the monsoon's path further east some five thousand years ago. There are some semi-arid parts of the Thar where animal and plant life flourishes, more so than in many other deserts.

The Turkestan Desert of central Asia has no rain between May and October, and its severe winter frosts kill many animals. It consists of two neighboring deserts, the Karakum and the Kyzylkum, located in the countries of Kazakhstan, Uzbekistan, and Turkmenistan.

The Ever-Changing Desert

A desert is always on the move. Even if it is not spreading, there is constant movement and change within a desert, caused by winds and moving particles of sand and earth. The desert's extremes of hot and cold can split rocks apart, letting the wind in to batter and re-shape them.

One of the most powerful forces shaping any desert is the wind. Hot winds in the Sahara and other deserts regularly reach 60 miles per hour (100 kilometers per hour). These winds blow away loose material, such as rock flakes loosened by the intense heat or cold, and carve and polish rock surfaces with sand grains like a giant sand-blasting machine.

The wind cannot pick up sand grains, but it can roll them along the ground. If they are rolling fast enough, sand grains bounce up into the air when one grain bumps into another. Once in the air, they are blown along by the wind before they fall to the ground again.

The dark and choking "sand storms" that occur in deserts are actually dust storms. Dust particles are much smaller than sand grains, and they can be blown thousands of feet into the sky. But blown sand stays close to the ground. You could sit in a chair and see above a sand storm if there were no dust particles also blowing in the storm.

Desert winds can clear sand from large areas, leaving boulders and pebbles behind. The cleared areas are called desert pavements. Ancient Peruvians made giant desert pictures by moving the stones to reveal paler soil beneath.

Sand Dunes

Dunes are formed when wind that is carrying blown sand slows down, or meets an obstacle. The sand falls to the ground as a small heap, but it doesn't just sit there. Unless plants grow to bind it, the dune can move across the desert at a rate of up to 50 feet (15 meters) a year. Sand grains are blown up the back slope of the dune, and tumble over the front or "slip face." Since sand moves from the back to the front, the dune keeps moving in the same direction as the wind.

The barchan is the most common type of dune. It is crescent-shaped, with its "horns" pointing downwind. Barchan dunes can reach a length of 1,200 feet (350 meters). The rather similar parabolic dunes are also "horned," but their long horns point into the wind rather than away from it.

Transverse dunes lie at right-angles to the wind, and occur where there is plenty of sand but little vegetation. Some transverse dunes in the Sahara are 62 miles (100 km) long. Longitudinal dunes occur where wind blows from two directions. They lie in line with the prevailing wind, and may be nearly 300 feet (90 meters) high.

Water in the Desert

Deserts are the driest places on the planet, but despite this they are shaped more by water than by wind. Water is a very powerful force, and an occasional rainstorm may have more effect on the landscape than months of wind.

A desert may go without rain for years, then suddenly receive a year's supply of precipitation all at once. When these rainstorms strike, flash floods rush like miniature tidal waves along dry watercourses carved by similar floods over thousands of years. These stream beds, which are usually bone-dry, are called *arroyos* in America, and *wadis* in North Africa and the Middle East. Fed by rainwater cascading off the hills and rocks above, each flood bears a heavy load of debris. The water is

Life-Sustaining Oases

Travelers in the desert must be aware of oases, as these lush areas can be vital to their survival. An oasis is an isolated area of vegetation within a desert, usually surrounding a spring or other freshwater source. Often, oases are formed when winds gouge deep troughs in low-lying areas, and expose underground water supplies that fell as rain in prehistoric times. The water that quenches the thirst of oasis visitors could be as much as 20,000 years old. The best known of these "fossil waters" is a huge supply, estimated to be 150, 000 cubic km in volume, that lies beneath the eastern Sahara, and is shared by Egypt, Libya, Chad, and Sudan.

Since ancient times, trade and transportation routes across deserts had to travel from oasis to oasis, so that supplies of water and food could be replenished. Thus people often fought to control oases, as they could therefore control trade routes and charge taxes to the people who used them. Oases are so vital to the economy of the desert that they often have walls to keep out the sand, and may be planted with date palms and fruit trees.

A Bedouin camp at an oasis in the Sinai Desert of Egypt.

Green shrubs grow in the bottom and sides of an arroyo, or dry waterbed, in southern California's Mojave Desert.

thick with silt, fractured shale, sand, gravel, and rocks. Even large boulders are trundled along the arroyo bottom by the force of the flood.

After a desert downpour the landscape is changed. The water soon disappears, evaporated by the fierce sun. But at the base of the hills, spreading wedges of muddy earth and gravel dry out into *alluvial fans*. The waterless arroyos have new sandbanks and new boulders. Within hours, seeds that have been *dormant* for years are sprouting.

In uplands, if there are no watercourses leading towards the sea, the storm water may accumulate to form an enclosed *playa lake*. Year after year, silt-laden water flows into the lake and evaporates, leaving minerals and salts behind. Over time the lake water becomes saturated with the minerals and salts, which make the water completely undrinkable.

The Great Salt Lake of Utah is an example of a large playa lake. The Great Salt Lake covers an area of about 1,700 square miles (4,400 sq. km), sitting in the middle of its own desert and surrounded by mountains. The lake is so salty that a person who bathes in it cannot sink—but the bather would come out of the water covered in a layer of stinging salt crystals.

Text-Dependent Questions

1. What is transpiration?
2. What are the four main types of deserts?
3. What is the world's largest "hot" desert?

Research Project

Choose one of the world's major desert areas. Using your school library or the internet, find out more about the desert. Write a two-page report that includes information on the size, climate, natural features, and wildlife that live within the desert. Present your report to the class.

 Words to Understand

annual plant—a plant that grows from seed, flowers, produces seeds, then dies, all in one year.

cold-blooded animal—an animal that must bask in the sun or seek shade to maintain its body temperature.

climate—the average weather in an area over a long period.

condensation—the process by which a gas or vapor turns into a liquid.

drought—an unusually long period without rain.

game—wild animals hunted for food by humans.

nomad—a herder who has no fixed home, but moves around with the animals between feeding sites.

pollination—carrying pollen from one flower to another, fertilizing it so it sets seed.

reservations—areas set aside for native wildlife or peoples.

sunstroke—a dangerous condition where the body loses its ability to cool itself down.

tuber—a water-storing plant root.

warm-blooded animal—an animal that maintains a high body temperature by using up food energy.

The thorny devil lizard of the Australian Deserts stays active in heat that drives most creatures underground, and hunts ants even in the hottest part of the day.

How Life Exists in a Desert

Deserts usually seem empty and hostile to life, but many deserts are home to a wide range of extremely successful plants and animals. These do not just cling to life. They flourish, in their own way, in some of the harshest environments on Earth.

Finding Ways to Survive

All plants need water. Without water, plants wilt, shrivel, and finally die. So how do desert plants survive in regions where it may not rain for years? They have solved the moisture problem by evolving in two main ways. They are either *drought* resisters, or drought evaders.

Drought resisters either store water, find it underground, or are able to survive on very small amounts of it. They are perennials—plants which live and grow slowly, sometimes for many years.

The cacti of the American deserts store water in their stems and branches. Many have deeply ridged and folded surfaces. When rain falls, cacti such as the giant saguaro suck up huge quantities of water through their wide-spreading, shallow roots. The roots must be shallow because most of the desert rainfall seeps only an inch or two into the ground. As the water moves up the stem, the folds between the ridges open up to make room. Some big cacti can store dozens of gallons of water.

Desert trees are also drought resisters, but unlike the cacti they often send down long roots to reach underground water supplies. The mesquites of the American deserts, as well as the acacia trees found in the deserts of Africa and Australia, have roots that extend up to 165 feet (50 meters) beneath the desert surface.

Some plants use fat roots called *tubers* to store water and resist drought. The tuber of the Namibian elephant foot yam can swell with water until it weighs 650 pounds (300 kilo-

Prickly Defenses

Desert plants are in danger of being eaten by wild animals, which seek the moisture they contain as well as other nutrients for their own survival. For plants to avoid being eaten, they have evolved a variety of defenses. As a result many desert plants have fearsome arrays of spikes, spines, thorns, and prickles—all of which can ward off a hungry animal.

Many desert plants, such as these flanking a normally dry stream bed in the Namib Desert, grow to maturity and burst into flower within days of being soaked by a rare rainstorm.

grams) or more. Another Namib Desert plant, the welwitschia, has only two leaves, which snake and curl over the ground for up to 70 feet (20 meters). Dew collected on these leaves is funnelled into the ground to be stored in the plant's large root.

Those desert plants which are drought-evaders are *annuals*—plants that grow from seed, flower, produce seed, and then die all in the space of a few weeks. The seeds of these plants may lie dormant underground for ten years or more until the right conditions, usually rainwater, set them off on a

Yucca plants are able to flourish in the gleaming gypsum sands of the White Sands region of the Chihuahua Desert; where their flowers are pollinated by yucca moths.

rush of activity. Many of these drought-evaders have brilliant flowers. This helps to attract the insects that *pollinate* them as quickly as possible before the blazing sun shrivels the flowers.

How Reptiles and Insects Survive

Cold-blooded animals, which include reptiles, insects and spiders, all have body temperatures that rise and fall with the temperature of their surroundings. This makes burning desert heat as much of a problem for them as freezing cold. Because of this, many desert creatures are most active in the early morning, evening, and night, and rest in the shade or in burrows during the heat of the day.

Many desert animals only become active after rare desert rainstorms. The rains are a busy hatching time for insects and other small animals, because their eggs hatch only if they come into contact with water, just like the seeds of desert plants. Eggs can lie dormant for years. In Australia, freshwater shrimps have appeared in puddles after the first rain in 25 years—having hatched from eggs that have been buried since the last rainstorm. Many insects have short, fast lifecycles like annual plants, passing through all the stages of their lives—hatching, feeding, mating, laying eggs, and dying— over the course of a few weeks while the desert is still green from the last rains.

Educational Video

Scan here for a video of plants blooming in the Sonoran desert of Arizona:

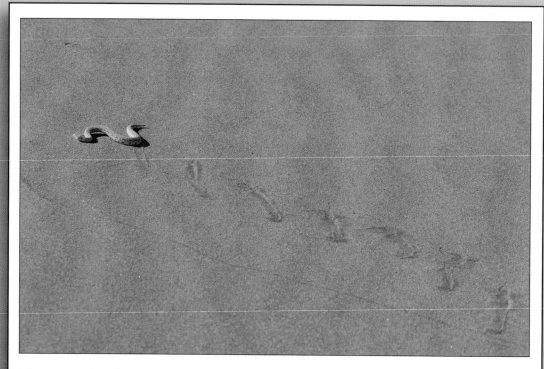

Like some other desert snakes, the dune adder of the Namib Desert moves normally over firm ground, but loops its body sideways over loose, sandy surfaces.

Desert insects get a lot of moisture from their food, whether vegetable or animal, but they may also find unusual ways of drinking. A Namibian darkling beetle obtains water from sea-mist. The beetle stands with its head down and its rear held high at the top of a coastal sand dune. The mist *condenses* on its wing cases, then trickles down into its mouth.

Although the highest recorded desert air temperature is 136°F (58°C), the desert floor regularly reaches surface temperatures of around 175°F (80°C) in summer. Close contact with this sort of heat could kill most animals in minutes. Some reptiles, including most geckos, avoid the heat altogether by being active only at night. Many spend the hottest part of the day in burrows. Others "swim" through sand beneath the surface, where it is cooler, as they hunt their insect prey.

Reptiles in deserts in different parts of the world have found similar solutions to the problems of desert life. Moving over a loose sandy surface is difficult for a snake, and the sidewinder viper of the Namib Desert copes with this by moving sideways over the sand, looping its body in a series of S-shapes. American sidewinder rattlesnakes and Saharan sidewinder adders use the same method to cross the desert sands where they live.

How Warm-Blooded Animals Survive

Birds and mammals are *warm-blooded animals*, which means that they generate a constant level of heat from within their bodies. This is a great advantage in a cold *climate*, but the birds and mammals that live in hot deserts need ways to get rid of some of their internal heat.

One way is to use radiators: large areas of the body that give off heat. The big ears of mammals such as fennec foxes and jackrabbits work like this. They have many small blood vessels, and the blood passing through them is cooled as its heat radiates into the air. The thinly-furred belly of a camel radiates heat in the same way.

Long legs are a big advantage in the desert, because the heat is fiercest at ground level. Gazelles and camels have long legs, and the air temperature around a camel's body can be 45°F (25°C) lower than the temperature around its feet.

Some desert mammals rely on sweating to keep cool. As the

The tiny fennec fox of the Sahara uses its huge ears both to listen out for prey and to help radiate heat away from its body.

sweat evaporates, it draws heat from the animal's skin, making it cooler. Unfortunately the moisture lost by sweating has to be replaced by water. A human in the desert can lose a liter of moisture every hour, and would be dead by the end of the day without water to drink.

Surprisingly, a thick coat of fur is a real benefit in the desert, because it insulates an animal against the intense heat of the sun. A camel has a thick coat on its back—but not on its belly—which keeps its skin relatively cool. This reduces the amount of moisture lost through sweating, and because the camel does not sweat so much, it does not need to drink so much. Camels are famous for their ability to go for long periods without water when not working—for two months or more in winter, and over two weeks in summer.

A camel also saves body moisture by not sweating until its body temperature exceeds 105°F (40.5°C). This is a unique trait due to camels' acclimation to the deserts—a human whose body temperature rose that high would be hospitalized with *sunstroke* and would be in danger of brain damage. Camels, and the saiga antelope of the Asian steppes, also have specially constructed noses which reduce the loss of moisture in their breath. Another life-saving feature of a camel is its hump, which stores fat, not water. The camel's body breaks the fat down into energy and a small amount of water. Fat-tailed mice use the same system in the Australian outback.

Birds can be successful desert dwellers, because their feathers are very good heat barriers. Even so, many birds stay in the shade during the heat of the day. The burrowing owl of the Chihuahua Desert in Mexico avoids the worst of the heat by staying underground during the day, and the elf owl of the nearby Sonoran Desert roosts in well-insulated holes in giant saguaro cacti. African and Asian sandgrouse use their breast feathers as sponges to soak up water, which they often carry long distances to their chicks.

People Who Live in Deserts

People have been living in the deserts of the world for thousands of years. In that time they have become experts at survival in these hostile regions. Although the impact of the modern world has affected the ancient way of life of these people, some still survive. Some of the most expert desert-dwellers include the Australian Aborigines, the Kalahari Bushmen, and the Bedouin of Arabia.

The last of these desert-dwelling groups to be discovered, during the 1950s, had no permanent homes and no clothes—in fact they had no possessions at all beyond their stone hunting weapons and the tools they used to gather plant food. What they did have was an enormous knowledge, built up over tens of thousands of years, of food plants, medicine plants, and the ways of the desert and the animals they hunted.

The Australian Aborigines are descended from ancient humans who traveled to Australia from Asia at least 60,000 years ago. Some became desert dwellers. The Aborigines were encountered by Europeans who explored and colonized Australia during the late eighteenth and nineteenth centuries. Unfortunately, for several centuries the Europeans marginalized, and often tried to exterminate, the Australian Aborigines, leading to a sharp decline in their population.

The San people, also known as Bushmen, have been hunting *game*, collecting plants, and surviving the savage heat of the Kalahari Desert for more than 70,000 years. They are probably the world's greatest hunters, able to tell from a footprint if the animal they are following is male or female, sick or healthy, young or old. Their way of life is harsh, but they are skilled survivors. They drink water stored by living plants, and cover themselves in sand during the heat of the day. Out in the desert they live in temporary shelters. Today, most of the San have now been forced to leave their hunting territories and live on *reservations*.

The Bedouin of the Arabian Desert are *nomads*, and live in tents. They often travel hundreds of miles between grazing areas and desert oases, with their flocks, their camels, their families, and their tents. A Bedouin tent is made from camel or goat hair, and is wide and low to the ground. Outside the tent, the Bedouin wrap themselves from head to toe in their robes and headdresses. This protects them from the dust storms of the desert, and saves their skin from the blazing sun. The Bedouin depend entirely on their camels, drinking their milk, using their skins and hair for their tents, and burning their dung as fuel.

  Text-Dependent Questions

1. How do drought-resistant plants survive?
2. How do drought-evading plants survive?
3. What are some adaptations that help warm-blooded animals survive in the hot deserts?

  Research Project

Research one of the desert-dwelling human groups, such as the San or Bedouin, using your school library or the internet. Write a two-page report about this group and the methods it has developed to survive in arid lands. Share your findings with your class.

 Words to Understand

commodity—a raw material or primary agricultural product that can be bought and sold, such as copper or coffee.

solar cell—a device that uses sunlight to generate electricity.

tungsten—a hard rare metal that is used in many electronic devices.

uranium—a dense metal that is radioactive and is used for generating nuclear power, as well as in weapons and in medical devices.

The Benefits of Deserts

For centuries most people thought deserts were useless—no good for growing crops, too hot for cattle, and too dry to live in, apart from a few wandering shepherds and their flocks. Then many deserts were found to be treasure-houses of valuable minerals including oil, *uranium*, and even diamonds and gold.

Oil in the Desert

During the twentieth century, petroleum oil became the world's most important fuel. The first commercial oil wells were drilled in the United States, but before long the oil companies discovered that some of the biggest oil supplies could be found under the deserts of North Africa and the Middle East. Suddenly many desert kingdoms, where wealth was once measured in camels and sheep, became fabulously rich in oil dollars.

The world's biggest open pit copper mine is located in the desert at Calama, Chile.

The demand for oil grew at a great speed. New factories and transportation systems, including cars, trains, ships, and aircraft depended on it. Oil took over from coal as a heating fuel. Natural gas, which is often found along with oil deposits, began to replace coal gas. Oil was also used in the manufacture of plastics, a gigantic new industry that emerged in the twentieth century.

Educational Video

For a 1959 news film on the discovery of oil in the Algerian Sahara, scan here:

Other Important Resources

Another valuable mineral found in deserts is uranium. Because uranium is naturally radioactive, it is used in the nuclear industry to generate energy. Like oil, uranium is difficult and expensive to get out of the ground, and it too has been found in desert sites. Desert uranium mines have been worked in New Mexico, Wyoming, and Texas. as well as in countries of southern Africa, Australia, and in the Gobi Desert of Asia.

For centuries Saudi Arabia was famous for the gold, silver and copper that were mined from beneath the sand. New mineral searches are revealing more of these metals, plus tin, nickel, chrome, *tungsten*, zinc, lead, phosphorus, iron, uranium, bauxite and potassium. Valuable minerals mined in other deserts include diamonds in South Africa and Namibia, silver in Mexico, and copper in Chile's Atacama Desert.

The rapid evaporation caused by desert heat also produces

large quantities of minerals. These dissolve in the water that flows from rock layers and soils when it rains, then reappear in mineral form when the water evaporates. They include salt, borax, nitrates, and phosphates. Chile has the world's largest known deposits of nitrate in the Atacama Desert. The largest phosphate deposits are in Western Sahara in North Africa. Nitrates and phosphates are used in fertilizers, which help crops grow in fertile areas of the world.

For countries that control desert resources, the citizens can benefit as long as there is demand for the resource and the national government uses the revenue for education, health care, power generation, or to create jobs. However, in these countries economic growth often depends on the price of the

The Great Man-Made River

One desert resource that lies deep beneath the surface is not a mineral at all. It is water. In Libya, water trapped in an ancient aquifer beneath the eastern Sahara Desert is being tapped in a mammoth project to bring water to the cities and irrigate parts of the desert.

Beginning in 1987, the Libyan government began spending billions of dollars on a project called the Great Man-Made River. More than a thousand wells were drilled into the aquifer, and over 1,750 miles (2,800 km) of pipes were laid in the desert. The project has continued to grow, and today it supplies 2.5 million cubic meters of water per day to many of Libya's major cities, including Tripoli, Benghazi, Sirte, and Tobruk, as well as hundreds of smaller communities.

Unfortunately, the infrastructure of the Great Man-Made River was damaged during the Libyan civil war that began in 2011. With the country in turmoil due to continued fighting between the various factions, the water supply for millions of Libyans remains threatened.

Deposits of salt, gypsum, and other minerals can be found in Death Valley National Park.

An array of solar panels in the Mojave Desert of Nevada.

mineral remaining at a high level. When *commodities* such as oil or precious metals experience large price drops, drilling or mining operations are often reduced, leading to job losses and economic hardships. This occurred with the price of silver in the late twentieth century, or more recently with the global price of oil, which has fallen sharply since 2015.

One plentiful resource that has not yet been used to the full is sunshine. For many years it has been possible to generate electricity from light-sensitive *solar cells*. Most hand-held electronic calculators are powered by them. In Saudi Arabia solar cells are set up on remote desert roads to power emergency telephones and electric signs. The Saudi authorities have even equipped several villages with electric power systems working off solar cells, and have used them in experimental machines to remove the salt from sea water.

In the United States, the first solar power fields were built during the 1980s in the Mojave Desert of Nevada. Today, there are a number of solar power fields in the Mojave. The largest is the Ivanpah Solar Power Facility, located 40 miles (64 km) southwest of Las Vegas, which opened in 2014. It is the world's largest solar-thermal power plant project.

  Text-Dependent Questions

1. What are three valuable minerals that are found in deserts?
2. What is the Great Man-Made River?
3. What is the largest solar power facility in the Mojave Desert?

  Research Project

Using your school library or the internet, research one of the minerals or valuable desert resources noted in this chapter, such as oil, uranium, tin, copper, tungsten, or gypsum. Write a short report describing the desert areas in which these minerals can be found, explaining why they are located in deserts, and what they are used for in the modern world. Present your findings to the class.

 Words to Understand

irrigation—introducing water to growing plants through channels or pipes.

nutrients—natural plant foods in the earth.

topsoil—the top layer of the earth, where many of the nutrients are.

overgrazing—grazing land for too long, or with too many animals, resulting in the destruction of plant cover and eventual desertification.

desertification—the process by which natural events and human activities reduce fertile land to barren land.

cash crop—a crop grown to sell rather than to eat or use on the farm.

predators—animals that kill other animals for food.

The Threat to Deserts

None of the world's major deserts were created by humans. A true desert is a natural system—and desert life, from plants to large mammals, has adapted to the conditions. But human activity on the edges of natural deserts has created conditions that have resulted in the expansion of the deserts. Unlike true deserts, the degraded, arid land created by human activities is practically lifeless.

About 10,000 years ago, humans began to abandon their life of nomadic herding and change to a more settled life as farmers. They cultivated crops and raised livestock on the Mesopotamian plain between two great rivers, the Euphrates and the Tigris, roughly where modern Iraq lies. The land was rich with river silt from regular flooding.

The early farmers grew wheat and flourished. First villages, then cities grew up on the plain between the rivers. Between seasonal floods, the land baked hard as rock, particularly in the south, so the farmers *irrigated* their fields with river water. But most of the water came from the slow-flowing Euphrates, which was saltier than the faster Tigris. They used too much of this water, and carried on doing so for thousands of years. The soil became choked with salt, and eventually—from a combination of over-irrigation, drought, and neglect due to frequent local wars—the land could no longer support plants. It had become more barren than any natural desert.

Choking Dust Storms

A more recent example occurred in the Great Plains states of North America's wheat belt. During the late nineteenth and early twentieth centuries, ancient grasslands with earth-gripping root systems were plowed up so the farmers could plant wheat and other crops. The crops were grown and harvested, year after year, without replacing the *nutrients* taken from the soil. The land was literally worked to death. The starved *topsoil* turned to dust, and the wind carried it away.

The worst-affected area of the Midwestern states became known as the Dust Bowl. In the 1930s the wind began to strip away the topsoil of the whole region. Skies turned as black as night, as millions of tons of dusty earth were carried eastwards and dumped far out in the Atlantic.

The Dust Bowl of the 1930s was created by a combination of exhausted soil and unusually low rainfall. Such natural droughts occur roughly every twenty years on the Great Plains. After 1939 the land began to recover, thanks to increased rainfall and greater soil care. Some areas of original prairie have even been restored by planting drought-resistant grasses. Low

A farmer and his children walk through a dust storm on their Oklahoma farm in the 1930s. Such storms removed huge quantities of exhausted topsoil from the Dust Bowl of the American Midwest.

rainfall between 1955 and 1957 brought the dust storms back, but with less damage.

Today, the same sort of thing is happening in China, where about 1,000 square miles (2460 sq. km) of land deteriorates into desert every year. China lies in the wind-path of the Gobi Desert, and years of deforestation to expand farmland have removed the barrier of trees that once held back the desert storms. Nearly one million tons of sand blow into Beijing each year. Most of the grass has disappeared from the once-fertile

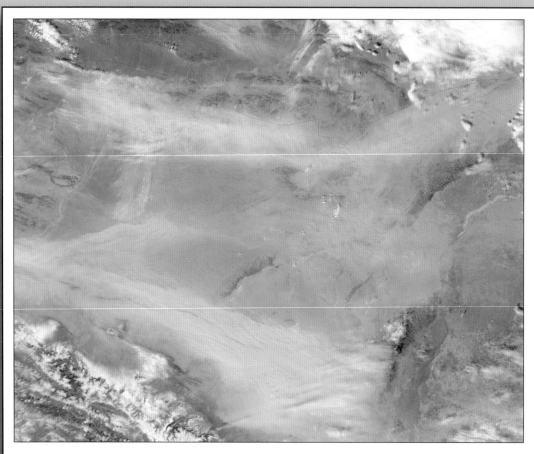

Two streams of dust can appear blowing from the Gobi Desert; the upper plume of dust is along the border between China and Mongolia. Winds often carry dust from the Gobi Desert eastward to Beijing and other populous regions along China's east coast, particularly in the springtime.

valleys north of the capital, and has been replaced by moving sand dunes. The sand destroys the food plots of corn, rice, beans and tomatoes which keep the villagers alive.

Scientists are concerned that Beijing may be silted over in a few years. During the1950s dust storms reached Beijing once every seven or eight years. By the 1990s they had become a yearly problem. In 2017, ferocious dust storms closed Beijing airport, and filled the hospitals with people suffering from breathing problems. Sand dunes are forming only 45 miles (70 km) from the capital, and may be drifting south at up to 15 miles (25 km) each year.

The Chinese government has begun a tree-planting project called "China's Great Green Wall," to take place over the next 70 years, and villagers have been signed up for the "green army." However, no one knows what to do about the sand.

Cutting Trees for Firewood

In the countries of the Sahel, along the southern fringes of the Sahara, firewood is being used up at least 30 percent faster than it is being produced. New tree growth cannot keep up with the firewood collectors.

In Niger, one of the Sahel countries, wood is the main fuel for over 90 percent of all households. Two million tonnes of firewood are burned every year, and it all has to be collected either in farming areas or in the "green belt" areas south of the Sahara.

Villagers find themselves competing with teams of firewood collectors from the towns, who travel in trucks up to 180 miles (300 km) from home in search of wood. The dead wood was finished long ago, and now living trees and bushes are cut down. When they die, the soil around their roots is easily stripped away by the harsh Sahara winds.

In western Sudan some villages are threatened by sand dunes which reach roof height. The Sahara is only 120 miles (200 km) away, but these dunes are formed from soil in the farming territories, which has crumbled and blown away because the trees that once held it in place have been cut down for firewood.

Feeding a Growing Population

Mongolia is a large but poor country, and its small population is growing at the rate of 1.7 percent each year. Three-quarters of the country consists of semi-desert grasslands on which nomadic herders graze their flocks and herds. There is little other agriculture.

As the population grows in the towns, where 72 percent of Mongols live, there is strong pressure to increase the size of the flocks and herds to help feed the extra mouths. The country now has 30 million grazing animals, far more than the land and traditional grazing methods can cope with.

Overgrazing has ruined some traditional herding regions, and sand has overtaken the tough grasses that the animals eat. Drought and overuse has dried up many of the wells, and some herders have had to leave the land. In places people have attempted to increase food-producing land by cutting down trees and plowing the thin desert soils. The results are disastrous, exposing fragile soil to extreme temperatures and strong winds.

Desertification

True deserts are formed naturally over thousands of years, but desert conditions created by humans develop much faster. Plowing, firewood collection, or overgrazing can transform a vulnerable area of drought-prone terrain into a barren waste-

The Shrinking Aral Sea

The Aral Sea of Central Asia was once the fourth largest lake in the world, with an area of 26,000 square miles (68,000 sq. km). Fed by two rivers, it had a flourishing fishing industry and a busy shipping trade. But in the 1960s huge new irrigation schemes for cotton plantations took 90 percent of the river waters flowing into the Aral Sea. The Sea began to shrink rapidly. The salt content of the water increased. Also, the new crops of cotton and rice were treated with enormous quantities of pesticides, which drained back into the rivers, and so into the Aral Sea. The fish began to die, and by the early 1980s the fishermen had all lost their jobs.

Today, the Aral Sea has shrunk to approximately 10 percent of its previous size. The exposed lakebed, now known as the Aralkum Desert, is thick with salt and pesticides. Every day strong winds carry thousands of tonnes of the dusty, poisonous mixture over the surrounding countryside, where it destroys crops and grazing land. The people who used to work on and around the Sea suffer terrible illnesses through breathing in the dust. Aral Sea dust storms have even been reported as far away as the Arctic.

The huge size of the Aral Sea disaster has had an effect on the local weather. There is less rainfall, and the growing season is shorter. The loss of the Aral Sea is considered one of the planet's worst ecological disasters.

land within a decade. This process is known as *desertification*.

For tens of thousands of years the Sahara region had a wet climate. Saharan rock paintings and engravings ranging over a period of 8,000 years show men harvesting grain and herding cattle. They also show wild animals such as giraffes and hippos.

The region where these pictures are found was fertile grassland for thousands of years, but after the last Ice Age, about 12,000 years ago, the Sahara began to dry out. Gradually, as rainfall and wind patterns changed, it became true desert. Today it has an average rainfall of only 4 inches (10 cm) per year.

Educational Video

To learn how the Sahara was formed in ancient times, scan here:

Like other true deserts, the Sahara is home to animals and plants that have had thousands of years to adapt to the heat and scarce moisture. However, desert-like regions that have been created accidentally by human activity have formed quickly, often within a few years. Neither plants nor animals in these areas have time to adapt. They die out or leave, so the "artificial deserts" are truly barren. They can recover if the rains return, but meanwhile they are almost lifeless.

For centuries the peoples of the Sahel region south of the Sahara had existed by herding cattle, growing crops and vegetables in village plots, and hunting. But during the twentieth century, the governments of Sahel nations urged their people to

Cattle Ranching in Australia

Australia is the world's driest continent after Antarctica, and agriculture occupies 60 percent of the total land area. Most Australian farmers are livestock raisers, and about half the total land area is used for grazing. Huge amounts of water are needed to support the sheep flocks and cattle herds, and because of this, Australia uses more water per person than any other country in the world.

Since the arrival of Europeans, about half the country has had its vegetation either cleared or thinned to make way for livestock ranching. Most Australian soils are shallow, salty and low in plant foods. They are easily damaged by overgrazing, and by the hooves of animals milling around artificial watering ponds. Trampled and compressed, the soils lose their plant cover. The root systems of grasses are destroyed, and the soils turn to dust under the hot sun.

Cattle ranchers often cram more livestock onto some ranges than the land can support, to try and make up the money lost by having underweight animals. But if more cattle have to share the same pasture, they just get even thinner. Many ranchers have lost everything due to this short-sighted policy, and have been forced to abandon their ruined ranges.

grow individual *cash crops*, such as peanuts and millet, to earn money from exports. Vegetable plots and grazing areas were cleared for the new crops. The herders moved their animals further north towards the Sahara, into drier areas with less vegetation.

The cattle became less healthy because there were too many of them for the scarce food in the dry territories. The new

In countries like Mauritania and Namibia, marginal lands that are adjacent to natural deserts have been have been degraded into desert by overgrazing and the introduction of intensive farming of cereals.

crops weakened the soil, which began to be blown away by the wind. As populations increased, people started cutting down living trees for firewood, removing wind barriers. And just when the people and their animals were at their weakest, the Sahel was struck by a savage drought. This combination of natural and man-made disasters cost thousands of human lives and millions of animal lives.

The Sahel drought was at its worst in the mid-1970s. By the 1980s the rains were returning, and satellite pictures taken in the 1990s were showing new growth of both wild vegetation and crops. But the droughts could return, and the story shows just how easy it is to create a desert by bad land management.

The Causes of Desertification

The desertification process begins with the loss of natural plant cover. The plants that protect the soil disappear—trampled by cattle, destroyed to make room for saleable crops, chopped down for firewood, or gnawed down to the roots by grazing goats or sheep. The earth is crushed by heavy tractors, repeatedly plowed, laced with pesticides and fertilizers, crusted with irrigation salts, and sucked dry by quick-growing cash crops. Soil surfaces become baked, then crumble. Natural events such as flash floods, sudden storms, or strong winds, which the land would have comfortably survived before the loss of the plants, finish the job off. The topsoil departs. Every year about 24,000 million tonnes of topsoil are stripped from the planet's surface like this. It is possible to reverse the process, and heal the damaged land, but that requires time and care.

The Effect on Wildlife

When a large herd animal virtually disappears we take notice, but desertification also destroys the small creatures which live at the bottom of the food chain. Without them, nothing else can survive for long, and with no animals to recycle nutrients, the land cannot grow healthy plants.

The addax is a type of antelope that is more highly adapted to life in the desert than any of it relatives. It can exist on a diet of tough grasses, and hardly ever has to drink. When no grass is available, it browses on spiny acacia bushes and herbs. It wanders great distances, mainly at night or in the early morning, seeking food. At the beginning of the twentieth century addax ranged over a vast area of the Sahara region. Now it is one of the world's rarest mammals, relentlessly hunted for meat, and no longer able to compete for grasslands with the ever-growing herds of domestic animals.

The African wild ass has also been reduced to a few small herds. It once wandered stony deserts and semi-arid bush from Morocco in the west to Arabia in the east. Now a few small herds hang on along the shores of the Red Sea. Its main problem is competition with domestic cattle and sheep for food and

Heat Extremes in Death Valley

The highest desert air temperature ever recorded was 134°F (57°C), in the Death Valley area of California. At one time, the highest temperature was believed to be 136°F (58°C) in the Libyan Sahara, but in 2012 this record was determined to have been a measurement error.

The addax is able to survive where most other animals would die of thirst, but now faces extinction throughout its range.

water. It has also been driven off or killed by the herders, who want the food and water for their livestock.

Large desert mammals are among the most obvious victims of desertification, but the process creates many less visible casualties. Insect grubs, worms and other tiny creatures live in the soil itself. They keep the soil in good condition by breaking down dead plants and animal waste into plant food. They also provide food for lizards, birds and small mammals. If these small animals cannot survive, then neither can the larger *predators* that feed on them, such as hawks, foxes, and wild cats.

When desertification is accompanied by increases in salt and poisonous minerals in the earth, due to excess irrigation, this also affects the water in wells and water holes. Anything that depends on these water sources, from toads and snakes to gazelles and zebras, either dies out or has to move elsewhere.

In addition to having their habitats cleared by farmers and destroyed by cattle and sheep, many smaller animals in Australia have declined in numbers because of introduced animals. The invaders either eat them, or compete with them for food. Cats, foxes and rabbits are among the main problems. One casualty is the bilby, a rabbit-like creature that eats seeds, fruits and bulbs as well as insects and spiders. It has fallen drastically in numbers, and its relative, the desert bandicoot, has become extinct.

Habitat clearance by farmers leaves such small mammals nowhere to hide, and they are easily picked off by predators. Both the fox and the rabbit were introduced to Australia to be hunted for sport, but both have multiplied in numbers to become major pests, as well as threats to native species.

Hunting in the Desert

Desertification and poverty are closely linked, because poor villagers are more interested in providing food for their families than in conservation. In the Sahara and Sahel countries, many animals are hunted ruthlessly. In Mauritania, which has suffered severe desertification, ostriches, dama gazelles, and oryx have been hunted almost to extinction by hungry villagers.

The same thing is happening in the Gobi Desert of Mongolia—home of some of the planet's most endangered animals. Many are killed illegally so the hunters can sell their body parts to Asian medicine dealers. The victims include musk deer, brown bears, saiga antelope, argali mountain sheep, elk, and snow leopards.

Desert life is harsh. Wild animals compete with one another, and humans and their cattle are competing for their share. People need food, and the wildlife they hunt often provides them with nourishing meat. The herder's cattle also need food and water. But it is not an equal competition. Cattle need more water than wild animals, and they destroy many of the plants that the wild animals eat. The herders would probably be better off in the long run if they tried to look after the land and grew a variety of food plants, but most of them know no other life.

Text-Dependent Questions

1. What was the Dust Bowl?
2. What is desertification?
3. What are some of the causes of desertification?

Research Project

In recent years, new dams have allowed more river water to reach the Aral Sea in hopes of restoring this waterway. Do some research on the current condition of the Aral Sea, and present your findings to the class.

 Words to Understand

erosion—the wearing away of earth, rock or some other substance by water or wind-borne sand.

evolve—the process by which living things change over many generations (also evolution).

perennial—a plant that stays growing in the earth for many years.

pesticides—poisonous chemicals used to kill insects, weeds, fungi and other crop pests.

sandstorm—a desert dust storm, with sand blowing along near ground level.

During the 1970s Dr. Wangari Maathai founded an organization called the Green Belt Movement, which has planted more than 40 million trees in Africa to combat desertification. She won the 2004 Nobel Peace Prize for her conservation work.

Addressing the Desertification Problem

Desertification cannot be cured in a few days. To halt the process and repair the damage takes knowledge and patience. Huge tree-planting schemes or heavy irrigation projects can make things worse. We are beginning to realize that the answer might be to address the problem in nature's way—slowly but surely.

The best way to stop a dune from moving or blowing away is to plant it with dune grasses or desert bushes. But how do you hold the dune still while the grasses are taking root? In oil-producing Iran, where over 80 percent of the land is arid or semi-arid, they spray a layer of crude oil sludge over the dune. This holds the sand steady and keeps moisture in. Seedlings are planted through the oil layer. The system seems to be working, and many farms have been set up in the dune-planting region.

China has 63.7 million square miles (1.65 million sq. km) of deserts. More than 22 percent of this wasteland has been created by human activities. *Erosion* rates rose steadily from the 1970s until the late 1990s. Worried about the sandy dust storms bringing the desert into Beijing, in 1978 the Chinese government began planting what it conceived of as a huge barrier of trees across the north of the country to keep the Gobi desert from expanding. At first, the project was an expensive failure, because a large area of the shelter-belt withered and died from lack of water.

Chinese scientists eventually determined that the worst of the *sandstorms* were coming from the human-created desert areas, and not from the true desert. They fenced off areas to be restored, stopped all cultivation and grazing in those areas, and sowed the ground from the air with drought-resistant grasses and shrubs. After four to five years, 40–60 percent of the test areas were covered in vegetation. The erosion was stopped by allowing nature's self-repair system a chance to work.

In 2003, China resumed planting forests at the edges of the desert, as part of what is sometimes called the Great Green Wall project. Today, the forested areas cover more than 200,000 square miles (500,000 sq. km), making it the largest artificial forest in the world. However, each year many of the trees planted die due to storms or drought. The government's current plan is to continue planting trees until 2050, at which point the forest will be 2,800 miles (4,500 km) long.

In other areas, patterns of water use have changed to make the deserts more productive. For example, when rain does fall in the Negev Desert, which covers 60 percent of Israel, the eroded hills funnel this precious water straight down into low-lying areas and wadis. By placing walled terraces in the lowlands, ancient farmers were able to use the runoff water to irrigate their crops. Modern farmers in the Negev are combining these ancient terracing methods with modern drip-irrigation, which enables them to use poor-quality water by delivering it to the roots, rather than the leaves, of plants. The combination of ancient and modern techniques allows Israeli farmers to grow a wide range of crops in some parts of the desert, including barley, wheat, olives, figs, and pistachios.

Preserving the Proper Plants

Like many crops, millet is an annual plant. It springs from a seed, grows tall, flowers, develops seeds, and dies all in one year. The seeds fall into the ground, or are carried off by birds, and become plants themselves in one or more years, when moisture makes them sprout.

Other plants are known as *perennials*. Their foliage may die back each year, but it returns the next season, and the plant gets bigger and stronger from year to year. In the wild, perennials such as trees and bushes hold the soil together with their roots, and protect it from erosion by wind or water. They protect the wild annual plants at the same time, and enrich the ground with their fallen leaves and fruits.

Throughout the countries of the Sahel in Africa, the land has been cleared of its natural cover by slashing and burning to make room for annual crops that can be sold for cash. Perennial plants have been dug up, so the annual crops have to grow without their protection. The Sahara winds kill the seedlings and keep the surviving plants small. The topsoil becomes eroded, and desertification results.

Shin oaks are low-growing shrubs that help to stabilize the dunes in Monahans Sandhills State Park, Texas.

One of the most effective ways to halt desertification and restore the land to fertility is to re-stock it with perennial plants. This is being done successfully in parts of Africa, Asia, and Australia. Local villagers have begun to realize that, with the protection of perennial plants, their crops will produce far larger harvests. Useful perennial plants with edible fruits or foliage can be planted beside crop fields, or in strips within the crop fields—providing food, shelter and, eventually, renewable supplies of essential firewood.

The perennials add food to the soil, and wild plants begin to return, providing soil cover to areas of the farming zone, and encouraging the return of wildlife species. Traditional water-saving methods are also being successfully reintroduced in Sahel countries. They include laying lines of stones across slopes, and digging numerous small pits; both allow rainwater to soak into the ground instead of being lost as runoff. The pits are also enriched with manure. So irrigation, artificial chemical fertilizers and *pesticides* are all unnecessary.

The Role of Governments

The governments of countries where desertification is a problem are often interested in doing something about the problem, but they usually tell farmers what to do instead of consulting them first. These orders from above often make desertification worse.

When governments of countries in the developing world borrow money from international banks, historically the banks have often instructed the borrowing countries to encourage the cultivation of cash crops that can be export to pay off the loans. So governments eager to borrow money order their people to grow annual crops such as peanuts and millet, which can be sold as exports. Large areas of perennial plants have been cleared by government schemes to make room for such crops. Villagers' needs for a variety of food crops that can be

Educational Video

Scan here to watch a short video on tree-planting initiatives in the Sahel:

harvested throughout the year, and land where they can hunt for game, are not taken into account, and neither is the risk of desertification.

As the extent of desertification has become more visible, local and international organizations have tried to deal with it in a scientific way. In China, where desertification is widespread, the Chinese Academy of Forestry has a Desertification Division which has teamed up with scientists from the United Nations Convention to Combat Desertification (UNCCD). One of their schemes involves the use of orbiting surveyor satellites to provide early warnings of desertification.

The UNCCD was set up in the early 1990s, to help countries with desertification problems. Today, 195 national governments plus the European Union are parties to the convention. Its stated aims are to get effective actions going. It wants to link local programs with support from international partners. It stresses the importance of involving local people. It states "Desertification can only be reversed through profound changes in local and international behavior." Every two years the states that have signed on to the UNCCD hold a conference at which they discuss activities. The most recent conference was held in 2017.

Looking Toward the Future

Organizations like the UNCCD produce large amounts of information about what causes desertification, and the best ways of dealing with it. However, knowing why something happens and what to do about it does not solve the problem. The theory has to be put into practice.

Some governments of arid lands may well be happy to team up with international partners to tackle their desertification. Such organizations can be very useful if they help poor nations to have access to expensive items such as satellites for monitoring weather, and computer programs that can make long-range forecasts about droughts and land loss.

But they may be less keen to be told their cash crops are ruining the land. Politicians are often unwilling to consult with the villagers, and many of them want to see their countries move away from traditional village life, and towards the sort of lifestyle enjoyed in wealthy nations. Most young village people would probably agree with them.

In the real world, however, such aspirations will not help the millions of people who are suffering from the effects of desertification. These people need simple solutions that address basic problems. For example, the over-collection of firewood has speeded up the destruction. It is now possible to obtain a cheap, efficient stove which burns far less wood, and this reduces the need for firewood.

Another problem is uncontrolled grazing. Effective electric fencing for livestock can be powered by solar energy, making it easy, and cheap, to control the movements of herds. It might also be possible to "farm" some wild desert animals instead of cattle. Early Egyptian farmers used oryx and addax as domestic animals. Unlike today's cattle, these native species have *evolved* to survive in desert conditions. They can thrive on a far rougher diet than domestic cattle, and do less damage to the vegetation. They can also go for long periods without water. Millions of cattle in sub-Saharan Africa die in the major

By using farming techniques that prevent desertification, village people in arid lands can work towards a secure future.

droughts that seem to be happening with increasing frequency, while native species are far less affected.

Education is one of the most powerful tools for fighting desertification. On the global level it is important that children in the developed, industrialized countries learn about the problems faced by children living where desertification is an everyday reality. On the local level, the children of the drylands villages need to understand the basic causes of desertification, and learn to apply the traditional techniques that can nurse degraded soil back to health. Better understanding, at both global and local levels, is essential for success.

Text-Dependent Questions

1. How can sand dunes be stabilized, or prevented from moving?
2. What type of plants can be planted in marginal, arid areas to prevent desert areas from spreading?
3. What is the United Nations Convention to Combat Desertification?

Research Project

Using your school library or the internet, research the Green Belt Movement founded by Dr. Wangari Maathai in the 1970s. What are some of the accomplishments of this program? What challenges did Dr. Maathai face? How does the program operate today? Write a two-page report with your findings and share it with your class.

Deserts

Adesert is a barren area where little precipitation occurs, making it hard for plants and animals to live there. Deserts are arid, meaning that they receive less than 10 inches (25 cm) of precipitation each year. Most people think of deserts as being hot and dry, but very cold regions of the Arctic and the Antarctic are also deserts, known as "polar deserts." These areas are extremely arid throughout the year because all their moisture is locked up in ice.

Hot deserts cover about 14 percent of the world's land area, or about 8 million square miles (20.8 million sq. km). Polar deserts cover another 1.9 million square miles (5 million sq. km).

The World's Largest Deserts

1. **Antarctica**, 5.5 million sq. miles (14 million sq. km)
2. **Arctic**, 5.4 million sq. miles (13.9 million sq. km)
3. **Sahara (Africa)**, 3.3 million sq. miles (9 million sq. km)
4. **Arabian (Mideast)**, 900,000 sq. miles (2.3 million sq. km)
5. **Gobi (Asia)**, 500,000 sq. miles (1 million sq. km)
6. **Kalahari (Africa)**, 360,000 sq. miles (900,000 sq. km)
7. **Great Victoria (Australia)**, 220,000 sq. miles (647,000 sq. km)
8. **Patagonia (S. America)**, 200,000 sq. miles (620,000 sq. km)
9. **Syrian (Mideast)**, 200,000 sq. miles (520,000 sq. km)
10. **Great Basin (USA)**, 190,000 sq. miles (492,000 sq. km)

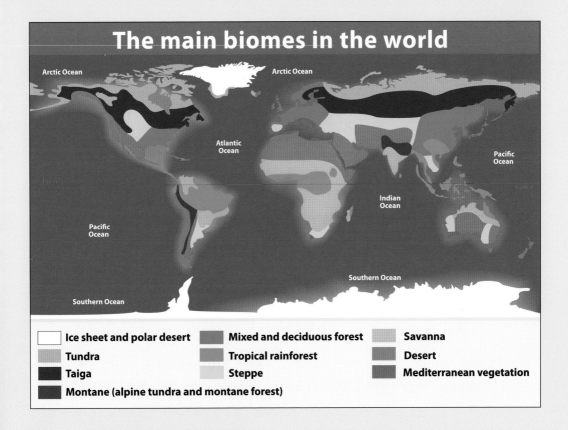

The main biomes in the world

Arctic Ocean

Arctic Ocean

Atlantic Ocean

Pacific Ocean

Indian Ocean

Pacific Ocean

Southern Ocean

Southern Ocean

- Ice sheet and polar desert
- Tundra
- Taiga
- Montane (alpine tundra and montane forest)
- Mixed and deciduous forest
- Tropical rainforest
- Steppe
- Savanna
- Desert
- Mediterranean vegetation

Desertification Facts

- Each year 46,300 square miles (120,000 sq. km) of productive land are lost because of desertification and land degradation, and the rate is increasing.
- United Nations, World Bank, and NASA figures show that 30 percent of irrigated land, 47 percent of cultivated rain-fed land, and 73 percent of rangeland lose some or all of their produce annually due to land degradation.
- The UN Food and Agriculture Organization says that 2 percent of the entire planet's land area is severely affected by land degradation.
- 65 percent of the African continent consists of deserts and drylands, and 75 percent of the agricultural drylands are in the process of desertification, according to the United Nations.

Appendix

Climate Change

The Earth's climate has changed throughout history. During the last 650,000 years there have been seven cycles of glacial advance and retreat. The end of the last ice age, about 11,700 years ago, marks the beginning of the modern climate era—and of human civilization.

Today, the Earth is experiencing another warming period. Since the 1950s scientists have found that average global temperatures have gradually risen by more than 1° Fahrenheit (0.6° Celsius). In the past, periods of warming and cooling have been attributed to very small variations in Earth's orbit that change the amount of solar energy our planet receives. Two things make the current warming trend unusual. First, most scientists agree that the warming is probably caused by human activities that release carbon dioxide into the atmosphere. Second, the speed at which the Earth's temperature is rising is much faster than this phenomenon has ever occurred in the past, according to climate records.

The heat-trapping nature of carbon dioxide and other "greenhouse gases" was demonstrated in the mid-19th century. Without the Earth's atmosphere, the sun's energy would be reflected back into space. Greenhouse gases in the atmosphere trap some of the sun's heat, reflecting it back to keep the earth's

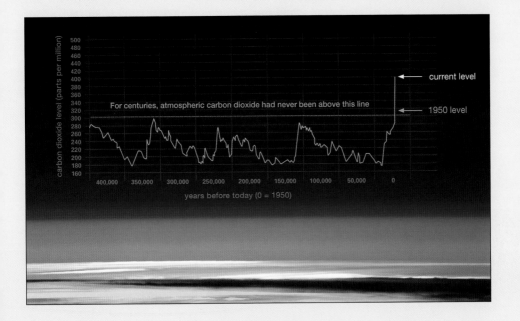

surface warmer than it would otherwise be. Without the atmosphere, the Earth's average temperature would be 0°F (–18°C). Thanks to the greenhouse effect, Earth's average temperature is currently about 59°F (15°C).

Increased levels of greenhouse gases in the atmosphere must cause the Earth to warm in response. Since the start of the Industrial Revolution in the mid-eighteenth century, human activities—including the burning of "fossil fuels" like oil, coal, and natural gas, as well as farming and the clearing of large forested areas—have produced a 40 percent increase in the atmospheric concentration of carbon dioxide, from 280 parts per million (ppm) in 1750 to over 400 ppm today.

Scientists understand how the Earth's climate has changed over the past 650,000 years by studying ice cores drawn from Greenland, Antarctica, and tropical mountain glaciers. Varying

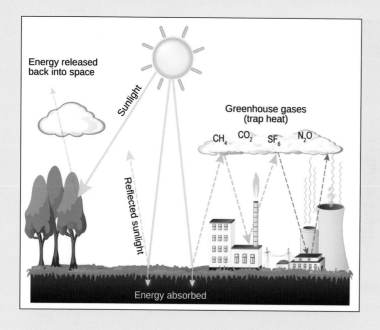

Energy released back into space

Sunlight

Greenhouse gases (trap heat)

CH$_4$ CO$_2$ SF$_6$ N$_2$O

Reflected sunlight

Energy absorbed

carbon dioxide levels found in the ancient ice show how the Earth's climate responds to changes in greenhouse gas levels. Ancient evidence can also be found in tree rings, ocean sediments, coral reefs, and layers of sedimentary rocks. This ancient, or paleoclimate, evidence reveals that current warming is occurring roughly ten times faster than the average rate of ice-age-recovery warming.

Most scientists believe that if greenhouse gas emissions continue at the present rate, Earth's surface temperature could grow much warmer than it has been in more than 650,000 years. Recent studies indicate that, if emissions are not reduced, the Earth could warm by another 3.6°F (2°C) over the next twenty years. This would have an extremely harmful effect on ecosystems, biodiversity, and the livelihoods of people worldwide.

Evidence of Climate Change

Earth's average surface temperature has risen about 2°F (1.1°C) since the late nineteenth century. Most of this warming has occurred over the past 35 years. Seventeen of the eighteen warmest years in recorded history have occurred since 2001, and 2017 was the warmest year on record.

Oceans have absorbed much of the increased heat, with the top 2,300 feet (700 meters) of ocean warming by 0.3°F since 1969.

The Greenland and Antarctic ice sheets have melted greatly over the past thirty years. Further melting of the ice sheets could result in significant rise in sea levels.

The strength and frequency of hurricanes and other extreme storms has risen along with global temperatures.

Series Glossary

atmosphere—an envelope of gases that surrounds the earth (or another planet). Earth's atmosphere, which is composed of mostly nitrogen and oxygen, helps the earth retain heat and reflect ultraviolet radiation.

biodiversity—the variety among and within plant and animal species in a particular environment.

biomass—the total of all living organisms in a given area.

biome—a very large ecological area, with plants and animals that are adapted to the environmental conditions there. Biomes are usually defined by their physical characteristics—such as climate, geology, or vegetation—rather than by the animals that live there.

climate—the long-term average weather pattern in a particular place.

climate change—a change in global or regional climate patterns. This term is generally used to refer to changes that have become apparent since the mid- to late-twentieth century that are attributed in large part to the increased levels of atmospheric carbon dioxide produced by the use of fossil fuels.

ecology—the scientific study of animals and plants in their natural surroundings.

ecosystem—all the living things, from plants and animals to microscopic organisms, that share and interact within a particular area.

food chain—a group of organisms interrelated by the fact that each member of the group feeds upon the one below it.

genus—a group of closely related species.

geodiversity—the variety of earth materials (such as minerals, rocks, or sediments) and processes (such as erosion or volcanic activity) that constitute and shape the Earth.

global warming—a gradual increase in the overall temperature of the earth's atmosphere. It is generally attributed to the greenhouse effect, caused by increased levels of carbon dioxide, chlorofluorocarbons, and other pollutants in the atmosphere.

greenhouse effect—a term used to describe warming of the atmosphere owing to the presence of carbon dioxide and other gases. Without the presence of these gases, heat from the sun would return to space in the form of infrared radiation. Carbon dioxide and other gases absorb some of this radiation and prevent its release, thereby warming the earth.

habitat—the natural home of a particular plant or animal species.

invasive species—a non-native species that, when introduced to an area, is likely to cause economic or environmental damage or harm to human health.

nutrient—chemical elements and compounds that provide organisms with the necessary nourishment.

species—a group of similar animals or plants that can breed together naturally and produce normal offspring.

umbrella species—a species selected for making conservation-related decisions, because protecting these species indirectly protects many other species that make up the ecological community of its habitat.

vegetation—ground cover provided by plants.

watershed—the land where water from rain and melted snow drains downhill into a body of water, such as a river, lake, reservoir, estuary, wetland, sea, or ocean.

Series Glossary

Further Reading

Clark, Mike. *Deserts*. New York: Book Life, 2017.

Dawson, Ashley. *Extinction: A Radical History*. London: OR Books, 2016.

Hansen, Grace. *Desert Biome*. New York: Abdo Kids, 2016.

Joppa, Lucas N., et al, eds. *Protected Areas: Are They Safeguarding Biodiversity?* Hoboken, N.J.: John Wiley and Sons, Ltd., 2016.

Kareiva, Peter, and Michelle Marvier. *Conservation Science: Balancing the Needs of People and Nature*. 2nd ed. New York: W.H. Freeman, 2014.

Kolbert, Elizabeth. *The Sixth Extinction: An Unnatural History*. New York: Henry Holt and Co., 2014.

Spilsbury, Richard. *At Home in the Desert*. New York: Rosen, 2016.

Taylor, Dorceta E. *The Rise of the American Conservation Movement: Power, Privilege, and Environmental Protection*. Durham, N.C.: Duke University Press, 2016.

Internet Resources

www.worldwildlife.org
The World Wildlife Fund (WWF) was founded in 1961 as an international fundraising organization, which works in collaboration with conservation groups to protect animals and their natural habitats.

www.audubon.org
The National Audubon Society is one of the oldest conservation organizations. It uses science, education, and grassroots advocacy to protect birds and their habitats around the world.

www.iucn.org
The International Union for Conservation of Nature (IUCN) includes both government and non-governmental organizations. It works to provide knowledge and tools so that economic development and nature conservation can take place together.

http://www.nwf.org
The National Wildlife Federation is the largest grassroots conservation organization in the United States, with over 6 million supporters and affiliated organizations in every state.

Publisher's Note: The websites listed on this page were active at the time of publication. The publisher is not responsible for websites that have changed their address or discontinued operation since the date of publication. The publisher reviews and updates the websites each time the book is reprinted.

www.fws.gov

The U.S. Fish and Wildlife Service is a branch of the government that is responsible for enforcing federal wildlife laws, protecting endangered species, and conserving and restoring wildlife habitats within the United States.

www.nmfs.noaa.gov

NOAA Fisheries is responsible for the stewardship of the nation's ocean resources, including the recovery and conservation of protected water habitats to promote healthy ecosystems.

www.nature.org

The Nature Conservancy is a leading conservation organization. It works in more than 70 countries to protect ecologically important lands and waters all over the world.

www.sierraclub.org

Founded by legendary conservationist John Muir in 1892, the Sierra Club is among the largest and most influential environmental organizations in the United States. The organization has protected millions of acres of wilderness, and helped to pass the Clean Air Act, Clean Water Act, and Endangered Species Act.

http://www.greenpeace.org

Greenpeace uses protests and creative communication to expose global environmental problems and promote solutions that are essential to a green and peaceful future.

Index

Aborigines, 30
addax, 52, *53*, 63
Africa, 10, 12, 13, 16, 22, 29, 33, 35, 36, 52, *57*, 60, 63, 66, 67
African wild ass, 52
Algeria, *11, 35*
Andes, 14
animals, *7, 8, 9*, 14, 21, 22, 25, 26, 27, 30, 46, 48, *49*, 50, 51, 52, *53*, 54, 63, 66
Antarctica, 8, 10, 14, *49*, 66, 69, *71*
Arabia, 9, 12, 30, 31, 35, 38, 52, 66
Aral Sea, *47*, 55
Aralkum Desert, *47*
Arctic, 8, 10, 14, 47, 49, 66, 69, 71
Argentina, 14
arroyo, 6, 16, 18
Asia, 12, 14, 29, 30, 35, 47, 55, 60, 66
Atacama Desert, 10, 14, 35, 36
Australia, 9, 14, 21, 22, 25, 29, 30, 35, *49*, 54, 60, 66

Bahrain, 33
barchan dunes, 16
Bedouin, 12, 17, 30, 31
Beijing, 43, *44*, 45, 48
Benghazi, *36*
birds, 9, 27, 29, 53, 59, 75
borax, 36
brine shrimp, *9*
Bushmen, *13*, 30

cacti, 22, 29

Calama, Chile, *34*
camels, *7*, 27, 28, 29, 31, 33
cash crops, 50, 51, 59, 61, 63
Central Asia, 14, *47*
Chad, *17*
Chihuahua Desert, 12, *24*, 29
Chile, 10, 14, *34*, 35, 36
China, *7*, 9, 12, 43, *44*, 45, 47, 48, 62
coastal desert, 8, 10, 13, 14, 26
conservation, 54, 57
continental deserts, 9
copper, *34*, 35, 39

darkling beetle, 26
Death Valley, California, 37, 52
desertification, 46-55, *57*, 58-65
diamonds, 33, 35
domestic animals, 52, 63
dormancy, 18, 23, 25
drip-irrigation, 59
Dunhuang, China, *7*
dunes, 12, 13, 15, 16, 26, 44, 45, 57, 60, 65
Dust Bowl, 42, 43, 55
dust storms, 15, 42, 43, *44*, 45, *47*, 58

Egypt, *17*, 63
Egyptians, 63
electricity generation, 38
Empty Quarter, 12, 46
endangered animals, 54-55
erosion, *41*, 58, 59

Numbers in **bold italic** refer to captions.

Euphrates River, 41, 42
evaporation, 7, 10, 18, 19, 28, 35, 36
extinction, 53, 54

farming, *50*, 60, 64, 69
    desertification, 8, 64
    firewood, 45, 46, *50*
fat-tailed mice, 29
fennec foxes, 27, *28*
fertilizers, 36, 51, 61
firewood, 45, 46, 51, 60, 63
flash floods, 16, 51
flowers, 23, *24*, 25, 59
fossil water, *17*
freshwater shrimps, 25
fuel, 31, 33, 35, 45, 69, 71

gazelles, *7*, 27, 54
giant saguaro, 22, 29
Gibson Desert, 14
Gobi Desert, *7*, *9*, 12, 35, 43, 44, 54, 58, 66
gold, 33, 35
governments, 36, 45, 48, 58, 61, 63
gravel plains, 12, 13, 18
Great Basin, 12, 66
Great Man-Made River project, *36*
Great Plains of North America,, 12, 13, 42
Great Salt Lake, *9*, 19
Great Sandy Desert, 14
Great Victoria Desert, 14, 66
Green Belt Movement, *57*

habitat clearance, 54
horse-latitude deserts, 8, 9

insects, 8, 25, 26, 27, 53, 54
Iran, 57
Iraq, 41
irrigation, 42, *47*, 51, 54, 57, 59, 61
Israel, 58, 59

jackrabbits, 27

Kalahari Desert, *13*, 30, 66

Karakum Desert, 14
Kazakhstan, 14
Kyzylkum Desert, 14

Libya, *17*, *36*, 52
livestock, 41, *49*, 53, 63
longitudinal dunes,16

Maathai, Wangari, *57*
mammals, 27, 41, 52, 53, 54
mesquites, 22
Mexico, 12, 29, 35
Middle East, 12, 16, *33*, *41*
minerals, *11*, 19, 33, 35, 36, 37, 38, 54
Mojave Desert, 10, 12, 18, *38*, 39
Mongolia, 9, 12, *44*, 46, 54
Monahans Sandhills State Park, Texas, *60*
Morocco, 52
musk deer, 55

Namib Desert, 10, *23*, *26*, 27
Namibia, *13*, 22, 26, 35, *50*
natural gas, 35, 69
Negev Desert, 58, 59
Niger, 45
nitrates, 36
nomadic people, 41, 46
North Africa, 12, 16, 33, 36
North America, 10, 12, 16, 42
nuclear industry, 35
nutrients, 22, 42, 52

oases, 13, *17*, 31,
oil, *33*, 35, 38, 57, 69
Okavango Delta, 13
Oklahoma, 43
oryx, 54, 63
ostriches, 54
outback, 14, 29
overgrazing, *41*, 46, *49*, *50*

Pakistan, 14
parabolic dunes, 16
Patagonia, 14, 66
Peru, 10, 15
pesticides, *47*, 51, 61
phosphates, 35, 36

plants, 7, *8*, 14, 15, 21, 22, 23, *24*, 25, 30, 31, 41, 42, 48, 51, 52, 53, 55, 59, 60, 61, 66
plastics industry, 35
playa lakes, 19
polar deserts, 8, 10, 66
poverty, 54
precipitation, 6, 7, 8, 10, 16, 66

rain-shadow desert, 8, 9, 14
reptiles, 25-27
resources, 35, 36, 39
rock paintings, 48

Sahara, 9, *11*, 12, 15, 16, *17*, 27, *28*, 35, 36, 45, 48, 50, 52, 54, 59, 63, 66
Sahel, 45, 48, 51, 54, 59, 61
saiga antelope, 29, 55
salt flats, *9*
San Bushmen, *13*, 30, 31
sand, 12, 13, 15, 16, *17*, 18, *24*, *26*, 27, *33*, 35, *36*, 43, 44, 45, 46, *47*, 57, 58, 60
sandgrouse, 29
satellites, 51, 62, 63
Saudi Arabia, 35, 38, 39
sea fogs, 13
sea-mist, 26
Sierra Nevada mountains, 10
silver, 35, 38
Simpson Desert, 14
Sinai Desert, *17*
Sirte, *36*
snakes, *26*, 27, 54
soil, 8, 15, 42, 45, 46, 51, 53, 59, 60, 65
solar energy, *38*, 39, 63, 68
Sonoran Desert, 12, 25, 29

South Africa, 13, 35
South America, 14
steppes, 12, 29
sub-Saharan Africa, 63
Sudan, *17*
Syrian Desert, 66

tents, 31
Thar Desert, 14
thorny devil, *21*
Tigris River, 41, 42
Tobruk, *36*
transpiration, 7
transverse dunes, 16
Tripoli, *36*
Turkestan Desert, 14
Turkmenistan, 14

underground water, *17*, 21, 22
United Nations Convention to Combat Desertification (UNCCD), 62
United States, 33, 39, 62
uranium, 33, 35, 39

wadis, 16, 58
water vapor, 7
watercourses, 16, 18
welwitschia, 23
West Asia, 12, 14
Western Sahara, 36
White Sands, Chihuahua Desert, 24
wind, 9, 11, 14, 15, *17*, *44*, 45, 46, *47*, 51, 59
 and desertification, 46-55, 57, 58-65

yucca plants, *24*

About the Author

Kimberly Sidabras is a freelance writer and editor. She worked with the World Wildlife Federation for nearly two decades. A graduate of Temple University, she lives near Philadelphia with her husband and three children. She is the author of five volumes in the WORLD'S BIOMES series (Mason Crest, 2019).